EBENEZER

Ebenezer

ISBN-13: 978-0692292822
ISBN-10: 0692292829

For information about production rights, contact:
www.jzettelmaier.com

Published by Sordelet Ink

Cover by David Blixt

EBENEZER

A PLAY BY
JOSEPH ZETTELMAIER

Published by
Sordelet Ink

EBENEZER received its world premiere in November 2012 at the Williamston Theatre (Williamston, MI). It was directed by John Lepard. Set Design by Janine Woods-Thoma, Lighting Design by Alex Gay, Sound Design by Tony Caselli, Costume Design by Karen Kangas-Preston, Prop Design by Stefanie Din. The production was stage managed by Rochelle Clark.

The cast was as follows:

EBENEZER: Arthur J. Beer
ALICE/HELEN: Alysia Kolascz
TIM: Joseph Seibert

Cast of Characters

EBENEZER SCROOGE - a businessman (retired), late 70s
TIM CRATCHIT - a soldier, 20s
MISS POOLE - a nurse, 20s

TIME
December 24th, 1863

PLACE
St. Bartholomew's Hospital, London, England

EBENEZER

*(Lights up. A nice room in St. Bartholomew's hospital.
EBENEZER lies on a bed. He is dressed in night-
clothes and under blankets. Next to him, sitting in a
chair, is MISS POOLE, a nurse. She's reading to him.
There is a coat rack with coats and a pile of presents
in the corner. The wind can be heard roaring outside.)*

MISS POOLE
"It was the day before Christmas; such a cold east
wind! such an inky sky! such a blue-black look in
people's faces, as they were driven out more than
usual, to complete their purchases for the next
day's festival. Before leaving home that morning,
Jenkins had given some money to his wife to buy
the next day's dinner.

'My dear...'"

EBENEZER
No, no. You must do a voice.

MISS POOLE
I don't think that's necessary.

EBENEZER
Oh, please.

MISS POOLE
Mr. Scrooge...

(EBENEZER uses a put-on, gruff voice.)

EBENEZER
Make him talk like this.

(Beat. MISS POOLE continues, using such a voice for the character of the Husband.)

MISS POOLE
"My dear, I wish for turkey and sausages. It may be a weakness, but I own I am partial to sausages. My deceased mother was. Such tastes are hereditary."

(EBENEZER chuckles at that.)

MISS POOLE
"As to the sweets -- whether plum-pudding or mince-pies -- I leave such considerations to you; I only beg you not to mind expense. Christmas comes but once a year."

(She looks up.)

MISS POOLE
Satisfied?

(She notices that he isn't paying attention.)

MISS POOLE
Mr. Scrooge?

EBENEZER
It doesn't, you know.

MISS POOLE
How's that?

EBENEZER
Not once a year. Many times. Many times a year.

MISS POOLE
My calendar might disagree with you.

EBENEZER
Trust me, dear. I know of what I speak.

(Beat. She goes back to reading, initially forgetting the voice.)

MISS POOLE
"And again he had called out from the bottom of the first flight of stairs, just close to the Hodgsons' door ('such ostentatiousness,' as Mrs. Hodgson observed), 'You will not forget the sausages, my dear?'"

(EBENEZER immediately turns to her. She sighs, then reads again, using the voice.)

MISS POOLE
"You will not forget the sausages, my dear?"

(EBENEZER smiles, perhaps claps a little.)

MISS
I hope you're quite pleased.

EBENEZER
I am.

MISS POOLE
Making a fool of myself like that...

EBENEZER
You read very well.

MISS POOLE
Only for you, Mr. Scrooge. Only for you.

(She kisses his forehead.)

MISS POOLE
Now get some sleep.

(She starts to leave. He becomes agitated.)

EBENEZER
Don't go.

MISS POOLE
I have to make my rounds.

EBENEZER
Please.

MISS POOLE
Besides, you could use a bit of peace. Been nothing but well-wisher after well-wisher for a week. Just lie back and...

EBENEZER
Please don't go.

MISS POOLE
Mr. Scrooge...

EBENEZER
What if they appear? I want you to see them.

MISS POOLE
See who?

(Beat.)

MISS POOLE
See who, Mr. Scrooge?

EBENEZER
Just sit down.

MISS POOLE
I asked you a question.

EBENEZER
Did you?

MISS POOLE
I did.

EBENEZER
Can't you just humor a sick old man?

MISS POOLE
You've got more life in you than a buck half your age.

EBENEZER
That's a lie. But it's a sweet lie, so I forgive you.

MISS POOLE
I promise, you'll wake up tomorrow.

EBENEZER
You don't know that.

MISS POOLE
Of course I do. I made a wish. And if Christ can't grant a wish made on Christmas Eve, then what sort of world is this, I ask you?

EBENEZER
It's only Christmas Eve for an hour more.

MISS POOLE
What?

(She looks at the clock.)

MISS POOLE
Ebenezer Scrooge! You've had me talking half
through the night!

EBENEZER
So what's one more hour?

MISS POOLE
It's the rest of the nurses working double-hard
because I...

EBENEZER
I paid them.

MISS POOLE
You what?

EBENEZER
Well, I paid your supervisor. Who then paid everyone else. You'll get your Christmas bonus in the
morning, courtesy of me.

MISS POOLE
Why would you go and do such a thing?

(Beat.)

EBENEZER
Charming senility?

MISS POOLE
You're senile like a fox, you are.

EBENEZER
Allow an old eccentric one last...um...eccentri-
cism. Is that a word?

MISS POOLE
Doesn't sound like one, does it?

EBENEZER
It most certainly does not.

(She just stares at him, deciding what to do. He pats the chair next to him.)

EBENEZER
Sit. Sit sit sit.

(She doesn't move.)

EBENEZER
You're alone tonight, yes?

MISS POOLE
I fail to see how that's your business.

EBENEZER
Well, you volunteered for the night shift. On Christmas Eve. And I heard Dr. Halsey refer to you as "Miss" Poole. Hence...

MISS POOLE
You're not currying my favor, sir.

EBENEZER
I can't help but draw the conclusion.

(Beat.)

EBENEZER
Although why such a lovely young lady hasn't found herself a husband...

MISS POOLE
If I stay, will you refrain from the... personal inquiry?

EBENEZER
I'll try, but it's doubtful.

(She smiles at him.)

MISS POOLE
You're awful.

EBENEZER
I am.

MISS POOLE
Utterly, terribly, irredeemably awful.

EBENEZER
But I'm also so very charming. Wouldn't you agree?

MISS POOLE
Only under duress.

(She sits back down, and picks up her book.)

EBENEZER
No more stories.

MISS POOLE
You're certain?

(He nods.)

MISS POOLE
Then what shall we do while we wait for your mysterious guest?

EBENEZER
I have no idea what you're referring to. And it's "guests".

(He takes the book from her hands.)

MISS POOLE
Hey!

EBENEZER
"Christmas Storms and Sunshine"? Feeling senti-
mental?

(She holds her hand out.)

MISS POOLE
I'll be feeling cross if you don't give me back my
book.

EBENEZER
One shouldn't speak of crosses on Christmas Eve!
You never know who might be listening.

*(He roles his eyes heavenward. She still holds her
hand out.)*

EBENEZER
Don't do that.

MISS POOLE
Don't do what?

EBENEZER
Don't hold your laughter back. I did that for many
years. Too many.

MISS POOLE
Perhaps I simply didn't find your joke funny.

EBENEZER
Oh. We both know that isn't true.

(She smiles slyly.)

EBENEZER
It's a start.

(He hands her the book.)

MISS POOLE
She's my favorite.

EBENEZER
Who is?

MISS POOLE
Elizabeth Gaskell. She wrote this.

EBENEZER
You're a reader then?

MISS POOLE
Oh yes. Very much so.

EBENEZER
Some men might be put off by that. Fortunately, I
am not one of those men.

MISS POOLE
Don't you start.

EBENEZER
Start what?

MISS POOLE
You're not the first old gentlemen to flirt with me.
You're not even the first one today.

EBENEZER
Oh I say!

MISS POOLE
Old Mr. Danforth down the hall? He was this close
to getting down on one knee.

EBENEZER
How close?

MISS POOLE
This close.

EBENEZER
Well! It appears none of us are immune to your charms.

MISS POOLE
Ha! There's a laugh.

EBENEZER
I'm being quite serious.

MISS POOLE
Charm isn't something I'm often accused of.

EBENEZER
Then clearly your other acquaintances aren't as perceptive as I.

MISS POOLE
They call me the Needle. Behind my back, of course, but I hear it nonetheless.

EBENEZER
Because you're so thin?

MISS POOLE
Because I'm cold, I'm hard, and I'm not afraid to draw blood should I need to.

EBENEZER
So others find you…prickly?

MISS POOLE
Just so.

EBENEZER
Well, that seems quite foolish to me. You are, without a doubt, my favorite of the nurses.

MISS POOLE
What did I say about flirting?

EBENEZER
No, no. That's God's honest truth. I was quite
happy to hear you'd be present this evening. In
fact, I requested that you be in this wing.

MISS POOLE
I know.

EBENEZER
Oh yes?

MISS POOLE
Dr. Halsey told me.

EBENEZER
The man never could keep a secret.

*(EBENEZER tries to sit up, but finds it difficult.
MISS POOLE helps him.)*

MISS POOLE
There now. Easy.

EBENEZER
Thank you.

MISS POOLE
How's the pain?

(He shrugs, saying nothing.)

MISS POOLE
If you don't tell me when it hurts, then there's not
much I can do for you, is there?

EBENEZER
There's not much to be done for me at all, so I'd
rather not complain.

*(The clock outside chimes quarter-past. EBENEZER
lights up.)*

EBENEZER
Do you hear that?

MISS POOLE
The clock?

EBENEZER
Quarter past.

MISS POOLE
Yes.

EBENEZER
It's almost midnight.

MISS POOLE
Don't remind me.

EBENEZER
They're not here! They have to arrive before...

MISS POOLE
Who?

EBENEZER
Who do you think?

MISS POOLE
Mr. Scrooge, visitation hours were done at eight.
Whoever you think is coming...well, they'll have
to come back in the morning.

EBENEZER
No! It's imperative! I don't have much time, you
see.

MISS POOLE
Enough of that talk.

EBENEZER
I wasted so many years. And now... it's all slipping
away from me.

MISS POOLE
This fear you're feeling...it's perfectly natural. You should think of...

EBENEZER
I do not fear death. No. Only that...when I am gone, everything I've tried to do stops. I can't let that happen.

MISS POOLE
There's no point in dwelling on that.

EBENEZER
I need help, I know that. But they haven't arrived and...

MISS POOLE
Who? Who hasn't arrived?!

(Beat.)

EBENEZER
I somehow doubt that you'll believe me.

MISS POOLE
I am a font of imagination, sir.

EBENEZER
I simply mean...I didn't believe it when it happened to me. Not at first. I thought it was indigestion. A bad bit of potato or some such.

MISS POOOLE
I had a lovely chicken broth for dinner, and a sweet cake after. Not a potato to be had. So out with it.

(He says nothing, unsure.)

MISS POOLE
Fine, fine. Keep your secrets. I'm sure whoever they are...

EBENEZER
They're ghosts.

(Beat.)

MISS POOLE
Ghosts?

EBENEZER
Ghosts.

MISS POOLE
Is that a fact?

EBENEZER
Oh, it's the very definition of a fact.

(He waits smiling, excited for her response. Finally--)

MISS POOLE
Time to go to sleep.

(She starts tucking him in. He pulls the blankets aside.)

EBENEZER
Don't you believe me?

MISS POOLE
...none of that now...

EBENEZER
They're coming! I know it in my bones!

MISS POOLE
Yes, yes. That's very nice.

EBENEZER
This is my hour of need! They must know that!

MISS POOLE
Mr. Scrooge, you need to calm down.

EBENEZER
They're coming! They have to!

(She stops, surprised by his outburst.)

EBENEZER
Miss Poole, they have to come.

MISS POOLE
I don't like it when you thrash around like that.
There's no telling...

EBENEZER
I have to see them one more time. Don't you
understand?

MISS POOLE
I'm sorry. I don't.

*(He stops, becoming confused. She can read it in his
expression, so she goes to him.)*

MISS POOLE
Mr. Scrooge, you're...you're not well. I think that,
perhaps, your mind is having a bit of fun with you.
I know that, in your head, this all makes sense to
you. But there are no ghosts. There's just you and
me.

(He struggles to regain lucidity.)

EBENEZER
Just you and me?

MISS POOLE
That's right?

(He looks around the room, sitting up more.)

EBENEZER
No...I can see it clearly...right there...he was like

a little boy, but like an old man, too.

MISS POOLE
Who?

EBENEZER
The ghost! The first ghost! He glowed with a bright light and carried a candle-cap with him...

MISS POOLE
Mr. Scrooge...

(He rises, going to the window.)

MISS POOLE
...lord help me...

EBENEZER
He took me out the window...took me back home....

MISS POOLE
Back to bed with you.

EBENEZER
I saw Fan...my sweet Fan...

(She leads him back towards the bed.)

MISS POOLE
Come on now.

EBENEZER
She was my sister. She died when I was...

(He pulls away, back to the window.)

EBENEZER
And Fezziwig's! He took me to Fezziwig's!

(He turns suddenly, with renewed energy. He grabs MISS POOLE in a waltz.)

MISS POOLE
OH!

EBENEZER
There was dancing! Oh and the food and the music! It was wonderful!

MISS POOLE
Put me down this instant!

EBENEZER
I had forgotten, you see? Forgotten what it was to laugh...to feel alive!

MISS POOLE
You're going to hurt yourself.

(He smells the air.)

EBENEZER
I can smell it...the spiced punch, the roast beef... and listen!

(He stops dancing, holding her by the shoulders.)

EBENEZER
There's music. Carols. They're singing Christmas Carols.

MISS POOLE
The carolers are long in their beds, sir.

EBENEZER
Listen!

(He quietly sings.)

EBENEZER
...I saw three ships come sailing in, on Christmas Day, on Christmas Day...I saw three ships come sailing in...

MISS POOLE
On Christmas Day in the morning.

(He smiles, turns her to him.)

EBENEZER
You hear it too?

MISS POOLE
I'm sorry, I don't.

EBENEZER
But you were...

MISS POOLE
Everyone knows that carol, Mr. Scrooge. I just got caught up in the moment.

(He wanders around the room, singing, searching for the source of the music only he can hear.)

EBENEZER
...And all the souls on earth shall sing, on Christmas Day, on Christmas Day...

MISS POOLE
Back to bed. Now!

EBENEZER
...and all the bells on Earth shall ring, on Christmas Day in the...

(He stops at the window. A surprised sadness hits him.)

EBENEZER
Belle?

(MISS POOLE goes to him, gently touching his shoulder.)

MISS POOLE
Be a good fellow then. Come on.

EBENEZER
I loved her. God, how I loved her. And I let her go.

MISS POOLE
All right then.

EBENEZER
My whole life…I never loved another…never… and I let her walk out of the door.

(He goes to the coat rack, looking for his coat.)

EBENEZER
…told me I loved only gold…that she was setting me free. She gave me back the ring, but I kept it! I…

(He stops, remembering. His sadness grows.)

EBENEZER
No. No. I didn't keep it, did I?

(MISS POOLE finally manages to lead him back to the bed, sitting him there.)

EBENEZER
I thought I did. But I didn't.

MISS POOLE
All right now. Just relax.

(He starts to cry a little.)

EBENEZER
I sold it. I was angry…hurt…I thought that, if money was all she thought mattered to me, that I…

(He looks up at MISS POOLE.)

EBENEZER
Why would I do that?

MISS POOLE
I'm sure I don't know.

EBENEZER
Why would I sell Belle's ring?

MISS POOLE
Listen to me. It's the past. That's all it is. We all do things we regret, but you can't let it stay with you. Selling a ring doesn't mean you didn't love her. Or that you don't still. All right?

(He nods. She takes out a handkerchief, cleans his face.)

MISS POOLE
There we are. No room for tears on Christmas Eve. Unless you're the Virgin Mary, of course. I imagine she shed a few birthing that baby, savior or no.

(He smiles a little at that.)

MISS POOLE
Now, will you be a good fellow and lie down before you give me a conniption fit?

EBENEZER
All right.

(He lies down.)

MISS POOLE
Shouldn't let yourself get all worked up by that.

EBENEZER
Yes. Of course. I…I don't know what came over me.

MISS POOLE
What's done is done.

EBENEZER
I must have given you quite a fright.

MISS POOLE
I've seen stranger. 'Least you kept your clothes on.

(He stares at her.)

MISS POOLE
Oh yes. Some things cannot be unseen, if you get my meaning.

EBENEZER
My goodness.

(They sit in silence for a bit, neither sure how to continue.)

MISS POOLE
Well, I know it isn't the day proper, but perhaps you'd like to open a present?

EBENEZER
That's quite all right.

MISS POOLE
Just one. I won't tell.

EBENEZER
Miss Poole, it is my belief that I'll be dead in the morning.

MISS POOLE
Don't...

EBENEZER
As such, I'd take it as a great personal kindness if you could have those gifts given to a poorhouse.

MISS POOLE
You can't stop, can you?

EBENEZER
I'm sorry. I know this talk of passing doesn't...

MISS POOLE
No, I mean...the giving. You can't stop, can you?

EBENEZER
Oh. That.

(He smiles.)

EBENEZER
Considering how long it took me to start, I'd say
I'm still making up for lost time.

MISS POOLE
For as long as I can remember, you've been the
heart of the city, sir. If you don't mind my saying.

EBENEZER
That's sweet, dear. But for most of my life, I was as
cruel, as covetous and as cantankerous a sinner as
ever walked the earth.

MISS POOLE
I find that hard to believe.

EBENEZER
Ah, the sweet ignorance of youth.

MISS POOLE
I'd wager there's not a soul in the old town that
hasn't been touched by your generosity.

EBENEZER
Even you?

(Beat. She goes to the presents.)

MISS POOLE
I'll see to it that your presents find good homes.

EBENEZER
Thank you.

MISS POOLE
Think nothing of it.

(She picks up a wrapped gift that is obviously a walking stick.)

EBENEZER
Whatever could that be?

MISS POOLE
One wonders why they even bothered to wrap it.

(She reads a card on it.)

MISS POOLE
It's from your nephew.

EBENEZER
Ah, Fred. Good lad. Wonderful lad.

MISS POOLE
I could tell. He adores you.

EBENEZER
And I him.

MISS POOLE
Thought we'd have to use a shoe-horn to get him out of this room.

EBENEZER
He's my sole relation.

MISS POOLE
I'd wager half these presents are from him.

EBENEZER
Oh no. Fred...lives within his means. Not to say
he's stingy, mind you. But the boy just won't accept
my help.

MISS POOLE
Then he's about the only one.

EBENEZER
It doesn't matter, I suppose. If I did give him
money, he'd just give it to someone he thought
needed it more.

MISS POOLE
Sounds like he takes after you.

EBENEZER
Would you believe that I actually took after him?
When I first decided to change my ways, Fred was
very much my mentor. Ah, if he were but twenty
years younger. And unmarried, of course.

MISS POOLE
Stop.

EBENEZER
I can't. Matchmaking is a favorite hobby of mine.

MISS POOLE
I beg you. Please stop.

EBENEZER
He's a handsome fellow.

MISS POOLE
Lord help me...

EBENEZER
If I had more time, I'd find you a proper husband.

MISS POOLE
Delightful.

EBENEZER
As it is, I suppose it will be your father's job to
find you one.

(She stares at him.)

EBENEZER
Did I misspeak?

MISS POOLE
I don't have a father. Or a mother. Not anymore.

EBENEZER
Oh. My dear, I'm so sorry.

MISS POOLE
You really don't remember, do you?

EBENEZER
Remember what?

*(Beat. She stares at him, uncertain if he's serious or
putting her on.)*

MISS POOLE
My parents were killed in a fire when I was 10.
I lived on the streets for eight years. Does any of
this sound familiar?

EBENEZER
Too familiar. London's streets are over-full with
unfortunates.

MISS POOLE
No...Mr. Scrooge. Look at my face.

(He stares at her.)

MISS POOLE
Is there nothing familiar about this face?

(He stares, trying to remember.)

EBENEZER
I'm sorry, dear. My vision is all but gone.

(She goes to him.)

MISS POOLE
I'm Alice. Alice Poole. And seven years ago, you saved my life.

EBENEZER
I did?

MISS POOLE
You did.

(Lights change. The sound of a busy tavern fills the room. TIM enters, dressed warmly. He places a ragged coat on MISS POOLE, who falls into his arms. EBENEZER rises, donning a coat as well. It is seven years ago.)

EBENEZER
Tim! Set her down there.

(TIM seats her, trying to get her to wake up. She does so, groggily.)

TIM
She's waking up.

EBENEZER
Good.

TIM
Poor thing's near-frozen.

EBENEZER
Then let's see what we can do about that.

(TIM wraps his coat around her.)

EBENEZER
See to getting her some soup, bread too. I'll stay with her.

TIM
Yes, sir.

(TIM rushes off. MISS POOLE stirs. EBENEZER sits with her.)

EBENEZER
There you are. Come back to us.

MISS POOLE
...where am I...?

EBENEZER
Dorry's Tavern. No more than a block from where you were...

MISS POOLE
What am I doing here?

EBENEZER
We brought you here.

(Beat. She pulls a small knife from her jacket.)

EBENEZER
Oh!

MISS POOLE
You keep your hands off me! Don't you touch me or...

(She breaks into a fit of coughing. TIM rushes over

with a glass of water. She drinks deep.)

EBENEZER
And the soup?

TIM
I'm just one man, Ebenezer! Give me a moment.

(He rushes back off. EBENEZER gently takes the glass from her.)

EBENEZER
Easy now. Slowly.

(She backs away from him.)

EBENEZER
I'm not going to hurt you.

MISS POOLE
Not like you'd tell me if you would.

EBENEZER
You have my word.

MISS POOLE
Oh! Well thank God for that then.

(She still holds out her knife.)

MISS POOLE
Old codger like you drags me to some dank pub, thinks I'm gonna...

EBENEZER
Ma'am, you fainted.

(Beat.)

MISS POOLE
I don't remember that.

EBENEZER
I imagine you wouldn't. But it happened nonetheless.

(She coughs again, drinks more water.)

EBENEZER
That's quite a cough.

MISS POOLE
Well, I'm quite the lady.

EBENEZER
I have no doubt about that.

(He points offstage.)

EBENEZER
That fellow there...he's a friend of mine.

MISS POOLE
So?

EBENEZER
You were picking his pocket.

(Beat.)

MISS POOLE
The hell you say.

EBENEZER
You had his pocket watch half-out when you
collapsed at our feet.

MISS POOLE
You got no proof.

EBENEZER
I would need proof if I meant to see you in prison.
That isn't my intention.

(She stares at him, uncertain.)

EBENEZER
What is your name?

MISS POOLE
What's yours?

EBENEZER
Ebenezer Scrooge.

(Beat.)

MISS POOLE
You're having me on.

EBENEZER
No.

MISS POOLE
You're Ebenezer Scrooge?

EBENEZER
You've heard of me?

MISS POOLE
Show me a Londoner who hasn't. You're Robin Hood with white hair.

EBENEZER
I...it's more silver than white, I thought.

MISS POOLE
You're the one that's kept half the charities in town alive.

EBENEZER
I suppose I am.

MISS POOLE
What good's that done me?

(Beat.)

MISS POOLE
I'm not like the rest, Mr. Scrooge. You done a lot of good, I know that. But did it save my ma and da when our shack burned down? Did it keep me out of the workhouse, or off of the street?

(He has no answer.)

MISS POOLE
If you want to peddle your charity, find someone else.

(She rises, but staggers from weakness. He helps her sit.)

MISS POOLE
I don't mean to spit in your face, sir. I'm just saying...I never asked no one for help in my life, and I'm not going to now.

(TIM returns with a bowl of soup and some bread.)

EBENEZER
I'm sorry for the hand you've been dealt. I truly am. And I apologize if I've made you uncomfortable. I just didn't want to leave you there in the snow.

(He rises, goes to TIM.)

EBENEZER
Come, my boy. Let's find a table.

TIM
But I just...

MISS POOLE
Wait.

(They stop.)

MISS POOLE
Is that soup for me?

TIM
And the bread.

EBENEZER
I wouldn't want to offend your pride with my offering of soup.

(Beat.)

MISS POOLE
Sit down already. I'm starving.

(They do so. She dives into the soup, talking as she eats. TIM tips his hat to her.)

TIM
Tim Cratchit.

(She offers a soup-soaked hand.)

MISS POOLE
Alice.

(He shakes it.)

MISS POOLE
Christ...I haven't eaten like this in a year easy.

TIM
I can tell.

EBENEZER
How long have you been on the streets?

(She shrugs.)

MISS POOLE
Years. Seven or eight. About that.

EBENEZER
Forgive me for saying so, but you'll not last another.

MISS POOLE
Oh? You're not just the Patron Saint of pinch-pockets? You're a doctor, too?

EBENEZER
You're frail, you're cold, and that cough would be dangerous for a healthy man.

MISS POOLE
If you're trying to make a point, you're taking the long road to get there.

(EBENEZER rises and walks away.)

TIM
That was rude.

MISS POOLE
My favorite opinions are solicited, Mr. Cratcham.

TIM
Cratchit. You speak well.

MISS POOLE
When the mood strikes me.

TIM
You are educated then?

MISS POOLE
Before my life went to Hell. I liked to read.

TIM
I was like you once.

MISS POOLE
Pffft.

TIM
It's true. And not just poor. I had the Rickets.

MISS POOLE
You?

TIM
Me.

MISS POOLE
You don't look it.

TIM
This was years ago. I got the medicine I needed, thanks to the man you just chased away.

MISS POOLE
I didn't chase him anywhere. He probably just had to piss. Old men piss a lot, don't they?

TIM
That old man saved my life. He'll save yours, if you let him.

MISS POOLE
Who asked him to?

TIM
No one. It's just what he does.

MISS POOLE
It's none of his damn business.

TIM
Mankind is his business. You need help, Alice. And you need it badly. Don't let your pride put you in an early grave.

(MISS POOLE stops eating, the reality of that hitting her.)

MISS POOLE
A fire killed my parents. Burned 'em alive. And I'd have been better off if I'd gone with them. A life like I'm living now...there's no good in it. I'm just...I'm just a rat that can talk. Sometimes, I think death would be...kinder.

TIM
Then you don't know what kindness is.

(He reaches into his pocket, producing a watch. He gives it to her.)

TIM
Here.

(She just stares at him, confused.)

TIM
You seemed quite intent on taking it not 30 minutes ago.

MISS POOLE
I don't want it like this.

TIM
Like what?

MISS POOLE
Like...like this.

TIM
It's better to have stolen it?

MISS POOLE
Yes! That way, I wouldn't have to...I...

TIM
Take it. Please. I'd rather it do you some good than just have it sit in my pocket all day.

(She thinks about it, then takes it.)

MISS POOLE
You're just like him, aren't you?

(TIM smiles at that.)

TIM
That's…I can't think of nicer thing to hear. Thank you.

(Beat. It's the first time someone's said that to her in years. She smiles and takes his hand.)

MISS POOLE
You're a good sort.

TIM
I'd like very much to be.

MISS POOLE
You are.

(EBENEZER returns. She immediately pulls her hand away.)

EBENEZER
Enjoying your soup?

MISS POOLE
I'd lick the bowl but for fear of splinters.

EBENEZER
Excellent. Because I have a proposition for you.

(Beat.)

MISS POOLE
A proposition for soup?

EBENEZER
No. For shelter. Mr. Dorry is that jolly fellow there.

He owns this establishment. It just so happens that he has a small room for rent above the kitchen. If you'd like it, it's yours.

MISS POOLE
How am I supposed to pay for it? In fleas?

EBENEZER
Your rent has been paid for. All you have to do is move into the room, and help Dorry with the cleaning.

(Beat.)

MISS POOLE
Don't do this.

TIM
What?

EBENEZER
I haven't done...

MISS POOLE
I don't want your kindness. I don't want it, and I don't need it.

EBENEZER
My dear, there is not a soul on this planet that does not need kindness.

(She is quiet, fighting a mix of sorrow and gratitude.)

MISS POOLE
I don't want your help.

EBENEZER
Yes, you do. You just don't want to ask for it. Now, you don't have to.

TIM
He's giving you a chance to start over, Miss. That's all this is.

MISS POOLE
You make it sound like such a...small thing.

EBENEZER
It isn't. I know that better than anyone. I also know how terrifying it can be.

(She says nothing.)

EBENEZER
I have stared at my own grave. I have felt the urge to step into it, to let the ground bury me. And every day since then, I thank God that I fought that urge.

(Beat.)

MISS POOLE
I'll stay here then.

EBENEZER
I'll let Mr. Dorry know.

(He heads off.)

MISS POOLE
Why would he do that?

TIM
A question like that can drive you mad. Just be grateful that he did.

MISS POOLE
I haven't had a home in years. I don't...

TIM
Alice. You'll be fine.

MISS POOLE
But I...

TIM
You'll be fine.

(EBENEZER returns.)

EBENEZER
I'm afraid we must be off, my dear. But let me introduce you to your new landlord first.

MISS POOLE
Oh, I...yes, of course.

(She starts to go, then turns to TIM.)

MISS POOLE
Will I see you around?

TIM
I'm afraid not. I've joined the Royal Navy. I ship out in the new year.

MISS POOLE
Oh. Well, then.

(She offers her hand again.)

MISS POOLE
Best of luck to you, Mr. Cratchit.

TIM
And to you, Alice.

(The lights change. TIM exits. MISS POOLE & EBENEZER are back at the hospital.)

EBENEZER
My God. That was you?

MISS POOLE
It was. Is. I…yes, I'm her. I'm Alice.

EBENEZER
I had all but forgotten.

(She lowers her head a bit.)

EBENEZER
I'm sorry. I didn't…

MISS POOLE
I understand.

EBENEZER
I meant only that my memory is not what it once
was. I remember that day. I remember you.

MISS POOLE
Oh.

EBENEZER
I should have checked in with you, I know. But I
felt that you'd resent any further intrusion…

MISS POOLE
You did more for me than any other. You never
have to apologize to me.

EBENEZER
That's kind of you to say.

(An awkward pause between them.)

EBENEZER
So you're a nurse now?

MISS POOLE
For five years. It still seems like a dream, sometimes.

EBENEZER
I'd imagine.

MISS POOLE
That winter...you were right. That cough was more than a cough, and was very nearly the death of me. Dorry sent for a doctor not a week later, and he saved my life as surely as you did.

EBENEZER
Dr. Halsey?

MISS POOLE
Indeed.

EBENEZER
Well...the old rogue can keep a secret after all.

MISS POOLE
I couldn't pay, of course. Nor could Dorry. But he offered me a trade, to help in the laundry here.

EBENEZER
My goodness. You worked your way from a laundry maid to a nurse?

MISS POOLE
I wanted to help people. That need can be contagious too, spreading from one person to the next.

EBENEZER
Are you comparing kindness to illness?

MISS POOLE
Having experienced both, I'd rather have the former.

EBENEZER
If only we had that choice.

(He lies back on the bed. She goes to him, wiping his brow.)

MISS POOLE
Mr. Scrooge, it is most unseemly to perspire so on such a chilly night.

EBENEZER
How bad is it?

MISS POOLE
Not so bad as all that.

EBENEZER
Alice, please.

(Beat.)

MISS POOLE
It could be better.

EBENEZER
I told you, I believe…

MISS POOLE
Yes, yes! I've heard what you've said already!

EBENEZER
There's no need to shout.

MISS POOLE
I just… For God's sake, Mr. Scrooge. You're not even trying to fight this!

EBENEZER
Of course I am. But it's not as simple as all that.

MISS POOLE
What of your nephew? What of your friends? Are they ready to be parted from you?

EBENEZER
I'm an old man. This is not new information to
them. But...no. No one is ever ready to let go of
what they love. It happens nonetheless.

MISS POOLE
It's damn selfish is what it is.

EBENEZER
Come now.

MISS POOLE
It is! I don't have a single soul who cares a whit
about me, but I'd still fight 'til there's no fight left
in me.

EBENEZER
You're still very young. But Alice...fifteen years
ago, I was given a second chance. I've lived long
enough to make some good of it. I have but one
task ahead of me now.

(He pats her hand.)

EBENEZER
But it's lovely to know that I'll be missed.

MISS POOLE
Half of England will mourn for a week. The other
half for a month.

EBENEZER
I've set up funds and charities. I don't know if it
will be enough, but...

MISS POOLE
It's not about the charities or the businesses or...
it's you, Ebenezer. The multitude of small kind-
nesses that you did personally, every day. So many

that you can't even remember all of them. Who
will do that?

EBENEZER
Why not you?

MISS POOLE
I...that's ridiculous.

EBENEZER
No it's not.

MISS POOLE
I'm not you! I'm just...me.

EBENEZER
I wasn't me either. That is...I mean, of course I
was me, but...A life changes because you choose
to change it.

MISS POOLE
It's not that simple.

(He chuckles.)

EBENEZER
In fact, it is. You just can't see it until you're on the
other side of it.

MISS POOLE
Pfft.

EBENEZER
Look how much your life has changed.

MISS POOLE
Yes, because of you.

EBENEZER
Because of you.

(She doesn't respond.)

EBENEZER
All I ever did for you was give you an option.
You're the one who took it. You're the one who
rebuilt a life. Never marginalize that.

*(Suddenly, the window blows open. A howling wind
can be heard.)*

MISS POOLE
Lord, what now...

(She runs to the window.)

EBENEZER
Wait!

MISS POOLE
You'll catch your death.

EBENEZER
I've already caught it. Just...listen.

(She listens to the snowstorm.)

MISS POOLE
I don't...

EBENEZER
There's a voice on the wind.

MISS POOLE
Yes. It's telling you to let poor Alice close the
window.

EBENEZER
They're speaking to me! Oh my dear Miss Poole...
they're...!

*(He coughs loudly. She slams the window shut and
goes to him.)*

EBENEZER
No...

MISS POOLE
Whatever else is going on, I am a nurse, Mr. Scrooge. And I'll not let a man freeze to death, even if he's already...

(She immediately changes the subject.)

MISS POOLE
So what did the wind say, hmm?

EBENEZER
Beg pardon?

MISS POOLE
Your howling wind there. You said it spoke to you.

EBENEZER
Oh, the wind didn't speak to me, dear. It simply carried a voice on it.

MISS POOLE
Fine. What did the carried voice say?

EBENEZER
Well, if you're going to be short with me...

(She glares at him, frustrated.)

EBENEZER
I'm afraid I couldn't make it out.

MISS POOLE
All right. Play your games.

EBENEZER
I would tell you if I could.

MISS POOLE
Of course.

EBENEZER
But when a ghost speaks....

MISS POOLE
There are no ghosts, Mr. Scrooge! I've walked this hospital for many years, and have seen more than my fair share of passing-ons. But in all that time, never once have I seen a single specter, spook, or spirit.

EBENEZER
Is it so hard for you to believe?

MISS POOLE
In ghostly visitations? Yes, I should say so.

EBENEZER
In anything? Anything at all?

(Beat.)

MISS POOLE
I believe in myself.

EBENEZER
An excellent start. What else?

(She thinks on it, but has no answer.)

EBENEZER
Is that why you're alone on Christmas Eve?

MISS POOLE
I'm not alone. I'm with you.

EBENEZER
Alice, I have only one regret left me, and it's that I never told Belle how sorry I was that I drove her

away. Don't walk through this world alone.

MISS POOLE
And what, get married and play the doting wife?
Do you know what I see when I come home at
night?

EBENEZER
What?

MISS POOLE
Everything exactly where I left it. All of my food
uneaten by anyone but myself. If I decide to go out
for a pint, I don't have to discuss it with anyone.
What do I need a husband for? To order me around,
to get him Christmas sausages?

EBENEZER
You've been reading too much of your Mrs.
Gaskell.

MISS POOLE
A good book, a nice fire and a hot toddy. That's
all I need.

EBENEZER
If you say so.

MISS POOLE
I do say so.

EBENEZER
All right then.

MISS POOLE
So no more discussion of a romantic nature.

EBENEZER
I'm flattered, dear, but you're much, much too
young for me.

(She laughs.)

EBENEZER
Ha! That's the spirit!

(The door opens and TIM enters. He's a young man wearing a military uniform and a thick winter coat.)

TIM
Uncle Ebenezer, I just....

(MISS POOLE lets out a little yell and jumps. TIM stops.)

TIM
Oh. I...goodness. Terribly sorry.

MISS POOLE
Who are you, and what are you...?!

EBENEZER
Tim! My good Tim!

(EBENEZER waves him over. They embrace.)

EBENEZER
Oh, my fine lad! How good it is to see you!

MISS POOLE
Excuse me...

TIM
Merry Christmas, Ebenezer.

EBENEZER
I thought you were still overseas. America, yes?

MISS POOLE
Please excuse me...

TIM
I've only just returned. I....

MISS POOLE
Excuse me, gentlemen!

(They turn and stare.)

MISS POOLE
I'm not sure what time the sun rises and sets in America, sir, but visiting hours have long since passed.

EBENEZER
Miss Poole, this is Tim, one of my dearest...

TIM
Ebenezer, please. It's Timothy.

EBENEZER
Of course, of course.

(EBENEZER leans in to MISS POOLE.)

EBENEZER
He doesn't like to be called "Tim" because it makes him feel young and childish. But I always say...

MISS POOLE
Tim or Timothy or Timon of Athens....Do you have any idea what time it is?

TIM
No, actually. I don't have a watch.

(She pulls out her pocket watch.)

MISS POOLE
It's half past Eleven, and I've spent the better part of an hour trying to get Mr. Scrooge to sleep. Your presence isn't conducive to that.

TIM
Of course, I only...

MISS POOLE
So kindly return in the morning, when St.
Bartholomew's welcomes visitors at...

(She notices TIM staring at her watch.)

MISS POOLE
Eyes forward, sir.

TIM
I'm sorry. I just...I once had a watch very much
like that one.

EBENEZER
Of course you did! Timothy, do you remember...?

(The clock tolls 11:30.)

MISS POOLE
And it appears the old clock tower agrees with me.
Out you go.

TIM
Please, just a moment.

MISS POOLE
How on earth did you even get in here?

TIM
It wasn't very difficult. The hallways are all but
abandoned, and most of the patients are asleep.

MISS POOLE
Then you should have no difficulty retracing your
steps out.

EBENEZER
No! Timothy, please sit down.

MISS POOLE
Mr. Scrooge, there are rules to take into consid-

eration.

TIM
EBENEZER
Yes, but you never really know if the rules work unless you bend them now and then.

(TIM goes to MISS POOLE.)

TIM
Miss...?

MISS POOLE
Poole.

TIM
Miss Poole, I have traveled a very long way to be here, and I would implore upon any sense of Christmas charity you might have to let me visit with my dear friend before sending me back out into the cold.

(She stares at him for a bit, then opens the door. TIM sighs and starts to go. Before he gets there, she stands in the doorway.)

MISS POOLE
I was just about to find a warm cup of tea. If you managed to sneak in while I was away...well, these things happen, I suppose.

TIM
Thank you.

MISS POOLE
You're welcome, Mr. Cratchit.

(She exits.)

TIM
Did she just call me "Mr. Cratchit"?

EBENEZER
Indeed.

TIM
How did she know my name?

EBENEZER
I...I'm sure you should ask her when she returns.

TIM
If she doesn't throttle me first.

EBENEZER
Oh, I think she likes you better than that.

TIM
Then you were witnessing a very different conversation than I was.

EBENEZER
Alice puts up a stone wall, surely. But if one gets close, they can see the many cracks.

TIM
"Alice" is it, you old rascal?

EBENEZER
You're never too old, Tim.

(TIM just stares at him.)

EBENEZER
Timothy.

(TIM sits next to him.)

TIM
You look well.

(EBENEZER laugh/coughs at that.)

EBENEZER
Come now. I may not have a mirror, but if my appearance reflects my condition at all...well, it doesn't matter. It was kind of you to say.

TIM
Here.

(TIM gives him some water. EBENEZER drinks.)

EBENEZER
What did Bob tell you? About my...situation?

(Beat. TIM isn't sure how honestly to answer.)

TIM
Father said you should've gone to the hospital a month ago.

EBENEZER
We both know I couldn't do that.

TIM
We do?

EBENEZER
I would've missed the Season. Unacceptable.

TIM
You should've come here at the first hint of trouble! My father could run Scrooge & Cratchit without you for a little while.

EBENEZER
Come the morrow, he will have to do that anyway.

(Beat.)

TIM
What are you saying?

EBENEZER
Tell me of your travels, boy! You've been gone for three years!

TIM
Ebenezer...how bad is it?

(EBENEZER takes TIM's hand.)

EBENEZER
You're a sweet lad to ask, but there's nothing can be done.

TIM
I'm sorry.

EBENEZER
Oh, it's quite all right. Every book reaches its final chapter.

(sensing TIM's sadness, EBENEZER changes the subject.)

EBENEZER
So how are your dear parents?

TIM
You saw them yesterday.

EBENEZER
So I did, so I did. But you know Bob...trying so damn hard to put on a cheerful face for me, never saying a peep about himself.

TIM
He misses you. We all miss you.

EBENEZER
Besides that, Timothy.

TIM
I think he's finally begun to accept himself as your partner.

EBENEZER
I would hope so! Adding his name to the sign should have given him an inkling.

TIM
You have to understand...he never thought of himself as a man of business. Just a clerk. You were the one who saw what he could become. Sometimes...sometimes it takes a while to see in yourself what others see in you.

EBENEZER
Of course.

TIM
Peter is helping him now. Did you know he'd hired Peter on?

EBENEZER
Oh yes. I suggested it, in fact. I felt that Scrooge & Cratchit might live longer as a family business.

TIM
Peter has father's gift for numbers. He's an asset.

EBENEZER
I'm sure there would be room for you there, should you want it.

TIM
No. I'm not a businessman.

EBENEZER
You're a Navy man.

(TIM says nothing.)

EBENEZER
Tell me of America. I've heard so many contrary
reports, I don't know what to believe.

TIM
That's understandable. It's a divided country, still
very much trying to find itself. Frankly, I don't
know that it ever will.

EBENEZER
You paint a bleak picture.

TIM
They're in the midst of a civil war, Ebenezer. The
country isn't even 100 years old, and already it's
coming apart at the seams.

EBENEZER
There's always hope, Timothy.

TIM
You always say that! You've been saying it ever
since I was ten, but...

(He collects himself.)

TIM
They're very different from us.

EBENEZER
The Americans?

TIM
Yes. They have...there's a fire to them. A great
passion.

EBENEZER
You're not calling we fine Britains passionless,

are you?

TIM
It's not the same. With an American...you never
have to wonder what they're feeling. It's all right
there, on the surface. They laugh easily, and they
fight just as easily. They love deeply, with every
fiber of their being...but they lack a sense of iden-
tity.

EBENEZER
You make them sound like children.

TIM
They very much reminded me of children.

*(Suddenly, the window blows open again. A gusting
storm is heard.)*

TIM
Good Christ!

EBENEZER
It's been doing that all night.

(TIM goes to it.)

EBENEZER
Wait!

TIM
It's freezing out there! Do you want it to be freezing in here?

EBENEZER
Give it a moment, please!

TIM
The whole damn room will be covered in snow if
I don't...

EBENEZER
Tim! Please!

(TIM just stares at him.)

EBENEZER
Just leave it for a moment. I beg of you.

TIM
You're mad. You know this.

EBENEZER
I do.

TIM
And I know there's always method to your madness.

(TIM moves away from the window.)

EBENEZER
Thank you.

TIM
Well, it's as good a time as any for your Christmas
present, I suppose.

*(TIM pulls a poorly wrapped present from his coat
pocket.)*

EBENEZER
I was actually just telling Alice, I'd rather have any
gifts donated to charity.

TIM
Of course you would.

(TIM begins to unwrap it.)

EBENEZER
I appreciate the kindness, of course. But there are
so many more in greater need than I that...

(The gift is a knitted cap. TIM puts it on EBENEZER's head mid-sentence. It looks a bit silly on him.)

EBENEZER
Oh. I see.

TIM
It'll keep the nip off your ears, at any rate.

EBENEZER
Thank you, Timothy. It's lovely.

TIM
That would have been more convincing if you said it after the lights had blown out.

EBENEZER
Those are paraffin lamps, my boy. It would take quite a gust to extinguish them.

TIM
The storm outside might be up to the task.

(EBENEZER holds his finger up, silencing TIM.)

TIM
Did you hear something?

EBENEZER
Shh!

TIM
I simply…

EBENEZER
Shh!

(EBENEZER listens intently.)

EBENEZER
…I can almost make it out…

TIM
Make...?

(EBENEZER glares at him. TIM holds his hands up in surrender & is silent.)

EBENEZER
It's a voice! I know that voice!

(EBENEZER rises & goes to the window.)

TIM
Oh lord...

(EBENEZER calls out the window.)

EBENEZER
You have to speak louder! I can't quite hear you!

TIM
No you don't.

(TIM grabs EBENEZER. EBENEZER shakes him off.)

EBENEZER
Tell me what to do! Tell me what you want me to do!

TIM
You'll wake the whole damn hospital!

EBENEZER
Tell me! Please!

(TIM slams the window shut, latching it tight.)

EBENEZER
No!

TIM
You have to calm yourself.

EBENEZER
What have you done?!

TIM
Kept you from falling to your death!

EBENEZER
I was so close! I could almost hear them!

(He clutches TIM.)

EBENEZER
Bring them back! Oh God please...I'm ready...I...

(He weeps. TIM holds him.)

EBENEZER
I want to talk to them. Why did you shut the window?

TIM
There's no one out there.

EBENEZER
Please ...I just need to know what to do...

TIM
I know you think you heard something, but...

EBENEZER
I'm not some befuddled dolt! There are things... God, Timothy....there are things that you can't possibly understand. Mysterious and beautiful things...and they came to me once, years ago. They showed me my past and...

TIM
Back to your bed.

EBENEZER
LISTEN! You have to listen. The man I was

before...Do you remember the Christmas fifteen years gone, when that great roast turkey arrived at your doorstep?

TIM
Of course. Father told us you sent it.

EBENEZER
I did. But...you see, the night before...ah, where do I start...Timothy, everything you'd heard about me up to that point was true. Every curse your mother uttered at my name was earned. I was as black-hearted and vile a man as ever walked the earth.

TIM
That doesn't matter, sir.

EBENEZER
It matters. Matters more than anything. Because you....

(His mood softens, smiling at TIM with great affection.)

EBENEZER
You never spoke ill of me. Not once.

TIM
How could I? I'm alive now because of you.

EBENEZER
No, before you'd even met me...before I'd changed...Even when others spat at my name, you never did.

TIM
I don't...did Father tell you that?

EBENEZER
He didn't have to. I saw it with my own two eyes.

TIM
What?

EBENEZER
The night before my redemption, a spirit...a
ghost...took me to your house. I watched your
whole family gather around the fire. You couldn't
see me, of course, but...

TIM
That's enough. Get back into bed or I'll call for a
nurse.

EBENEZER
Your father tried to toast me, but your mother
protested. Said she'd give me a piece of her mind
and hoped I'd choke on it. But you...you raised
your glass to me. All of ten years old, you raised
your little glass and toasted me.

TIM
Why are you telling me this?

EBENEZER
And slowly...one by one...your brothers, sisters...
your mother and father...all raised their glasses
too. And do you remember what you said then?

TIM
That was a long time ago, Uncle Ebenezer. I
don't...

EBENEZER
You do! You have to remember!

TIM
So much has happened since then. You can't
expect me to remember one Christmas Eve out
of so many.

(EBENEZER laughs.)

EBENEZER
Lord love you, but you're a terrible liar, Tim. Always were. You know what you said. "God bless..."

(EBENEZER's weakness catches up to him & he falters. TIM helps him sit on the bed.)

TIM
Uncle, you shouldn't agitate yourself like this.

EBENEZER
I always appreciated that affection, Tim. "Uncle." I couldn't love you more if you were my own flesh and blood.

(TIM backs away, wrestling with his emotions.)

EBENEZER
Tim?

TIM
Timothy. How many times must I tell you? Timothy.

EBENEZER
I've upset you. I'm sorry. I didn't...

TIM
I'm not a boy! That's all I'm saying, Ebenezer. I just...you look at me, and you see the crippled child I was. The tiny lad you carried on your shoulders and...I'm not him! Why can't you see that?

EBENEZER
You will always be that boy to me.

TIM
Don't! Don't say that.

EBENEZER
Whatever else, to me...you're still Tiny Tim.

TIM
No! Don't bloody say that! Don't...!

(TIM paces, trying to hold back his anger.)

TIM
I just wanted to see you one more time. That's all. To sit at your bedside and to remember better times. Why do you have to make it so damn difficult?

EBENEZER
My boy, what is it?

TIM
You have no idea. The world you've spent so much time trying to brighten, it didn't even notice. All the good you've done in London...go fifty miles in any direction and it means nothing.

EBENEZER
That's not you talking.

TIM
It's not the Tim you remember, but it's Tim nonetheless.

EBENEZER
Has being an officer changed you so much?

TIM
I'm not an officer!

(Beat. EBENEZER stares at him.)

TIM
Not for much longer.

EBENEZER
What happened?

TIM
The world happened. As it always happens.

(TIM sits by the Christmas Tree. He inspects the presents as he speaks.)

TIM
Have you ever heard of Thanksgiving?

(EBENEZER shakes his head "no".)

TIM
An American holiday celebrating…it's hard to say. They celebrate every damn thing. This year, their President proclaimed it a national holiday. A day to be thankful for their country's great bounty.

EBENEZER
There's nothing wrong with celebrating, Timothy. The world would be a merrier place if we had more of it.

TIM
Doesn't it seem odd, though? Setting up a holiday in the middle of this great war?

EBENEZER
Perhaps that's when a sense of hope is most needed.

TIM
Hope? Christ almighty, I don't know that I'd even recognize hope if I saw it.

(TIM looks up at EBENEZER.)

TIM
The truth is, we don't all deserve God's blessing.

(The lights change. The setting is the kitchen in a mansion in Mississippi, a month earlier. TIM is walking about with a candle. HELEN, a kitchen maid, is loading food into a basket. She stops.)

HELEN
Who's there? Is somebody there?

TIM
I'm sorry. I didn't mean...

HELEN
Oh! Leftenant, I didn't realize...

TIM
Perhaps you could...

HELEN
Just give me a moment to clean up and...

(She puts the basket under the table as he enters.)

TIM
It's Helen, yes?

HELEN
Leftenant.

TIM
Timothy. Please.

HELEN
Sir.

TIM
Could you help me please? I was looking for the kitchen and...

(She just stares at him.)

TIM
I was hoping there might be some pie left.

(She continues to just stare at him.)

TIM
It's a terrible habit, I know. Ever since I was a child, I've always been ravenous in the evening. And the feast tonight was truly exceptional and I...

(TIM looks around.)

TIM
I am in the kitchen, aren't I?

HELEN
You are.

TIM
Well. Apparently my gullet sees better than my eyes.

HELEN
Yes. Well. Let me just clean this up....

TIM
Please, let me help.

(He sits, begins eating.)

TIM
This is quite a place.

HELEN
One of Virginia's finest.

TIM
Have you been in Mr. Comstock's service long?

HELEN
Since I was a girl.

TIM
Ah. Are all his gatherings so...lavish?

HELEN
No, sir. Mr. Comstock enjoys celebrating holidays, even the ones endorsed by Lincoln.

TIM
I see.

HELEN
And having you and the Ambassador here...He wanted to make a good showing.

(Beat.)

HELEN
Did he make a good showing?

TIM
Hard to say. The Ambassador is a difficult man to read.

HELEN
But you're his...I'm sorry, I forget the word.

TIM
Attaché?

HELEN
Yes.

TIM
I'm not, actually. Captain Halliwell is the Military Attaché. And I'm the Captain's assistant.

HELEN
Of course.

TIM
In fact, you might say we're both servants. Please,

join me.

HELEN
I really shouldn't. I...

TIM
Is that stuffing?

(TIM digs in ravenously. She laughs a little. TIM looks up.)

HELEN
I'm sorry. I just thought.... I imagined all Englishmen to be very...proper.

TIM
I'm eating like a wolf bringing down a deer, aren't I?

HELEN
It's all right.

TIM
My appetite got the better of my manners. But please don't let it besmirch your opinion of the English.

HELEN
Actually, I think they've improved my opinion.

TIM
Excellent.

(He wipes his mouth on his sleeve. She laughs again.)

HELEN
Is it true what they say?

TIM
That depends. What do they say?

HELEN
Is Britain going to recognize the Confederacy as
its own country?

(TIM *shrugs as he eats.*)

HELEN
Is that a yes or a no?

TIM
It's not my place to say.

HELEN
Oh.

TIM
I'm only here to assist the Captain. I don't attend
the more important meetings.

HELEN
But the Ambassador is here.

TIM
Yes he is.

HELEN
I can't help but draw the conclusion.

TIM
I'd say more if I could.

HELEN
But you can't.

TIM
But I can't.

HELEN
The South could certainly use Britain's support.
And supplies.

TIM
And I could use a plate that never runs out of pie.
Some prayers go unanswered.

HELEN
So the meetings aren't going well?

TIM
I didn't say that.

HELEN
No. Of course. Pardon me.

(She smiles a bit. TIM catches it.)

TIM
That pleases you?

HELEN
Hmm?

TIM
That the talks aren't progressing as Comstock
would like them to.

HELEN
I don't have an opinion on it, sir.

TIM
I find that very hard to believe.

HELEN
I'm just a kitchen girl.

TIM
Who asks a lot of questions. And smiles at the news
she's glad to hear.

HELEN
I didn't...I was smiling about something else.

TIM
You have no love for the Confederacy.

(She says nothing.)

TIM
I'll let you in on a secret. Neither do I.

HELEN
Truly?

TIM
I don't care for slavery.

(She looks around nervously.)

HELEN
I wouldn't say that too loudly.

TIM
The house is asleep. Besides, I'm a guest.

HELEN
That sort of thinking isn't popular around here.

TIM
And yet, you think it. *(rising, bumping his foot on the basket. He stares at it.)* This food isn't for me, is it?

HELEN
Of course it is. I...

TIM
You weren't cleaning the table. You were packing this food up. Which makes me wonder who this feast is for.

(Beat. She says nothing.)

TIM
Helen, what's wrong?

HELEN
Did you mean what you said? About your feelings
for the Confederacy?

TIM
Yes.

HELEN
Then please, just go back to your room and forget
you ever saw me.

TIM
Are you in danger?

HELEN
We're all in danger. Each and every one of us.

(Beat.)

HELEN
There is a group of men about a half mile into the
forest, just past the manor house.

TIM
The people you were bringing the food to?

HELEN
Union sympathizers. Mr. Comstock's slaves are
with them now.

TIM
Dear God.

HELEN
I had to do something! I have friends among them
and I knew Comstock would drink himself into a
stupor tonight.

TIM
If he catches you, he'll...

HELEN
I know.

TIM
Then why in God's name...

HELEN
A countryman of yours once said, "All that is required for evil to prevail is for good men to do nothing."

(Beat.)

TIM
You have to get out of here.

HELEN
I was trying to do just that. Somehow, my plan was interrupted.

(He digs some money out of his pocket.)

TIM
Here. I don't have much American currency, but take it.

HELEN
If Comstock discovers you helped me...

TIM
He won't. And even if he did, he'd never lift a finger. He wants my country's help too dearly.

HELEN
You don't even know me.

TIM
I know you had a choice, and you chose something over nothing.

HELEN
Thank you.

TIM
You can thank me by leaving with all haste.

(She starts to go, then runs back and hugs TIM. He is momentarily stunned, and half-hugs her back.)

HELEN
Goodbye, Leftenant.

TIM
Goodbye, Helen.

(She runs off. Lights return us to the hospital room.)

TIM
Comstock's men found them the next day. He had them all shot.

EBENEZER
Oh God.

TIM
The slaves, the Union men and Helen. All dead.

EBENEZER
My boy, I'm so sorry.

TIM
And when I arrived home...I'm not a soldier anymore, Uncle.

EBENEZER
Tim...

(He tries to rise, but is too weak. TIM helps him lie back down.)

TIM
I shouldn't have told you.

EBENEZER
It was good that you did. That's too great a burden to bear alone.

TIM
They were hunted down like animals! This woman...this poor woman saw injustice and acted! She asked for nothing, she just listened to her conscience and she lost everything because of it.

(TIM fights his tears.)

TIM
I have wanted to be like you since I was ten years old. My God, I joined the Navy because I wanted to serve England in my own way, just as you did in yours. I was going to see the world, and bring with me the same kindness you've always given others...but that world is a lie, Ebenezer. This world...THIS world...

EBENEZER
Tim...

TIM
Everywhere I went, I saw the same thing. Men in power, using their influence to turn one against another. Men who truly believed themselves good, rising up against their neighbors for the sin of looking differently, thinking differently. There is no peace on earth, just intolerance and fear and...

(EBENEZER rises, shaky. TIM goes to him.)

TIM
What are you doing?

EBENEZER
You're wrong, Tim.

TIM
Lord, you're burning up.

EBENEZER
Listen to me, please...

TIM
Miss Poole! My Uncle is...

(EBENEZER claps a hand over TIM's mouth.)

EBENEZER
You have to listen to me, Tim. I know with great certainty that I am not long for this world, but so help me, I will not leave it until you have heard me out. So be...quiet.

(EBENEZER removes his hand.)

EBENEZER
That world you speak of...I helped to make it. For much of my life, I spread sorrow and hatred like a sickness. Everything I've done for the last fifteen years, I did to...to...

(His weakness catches up with him, and he falters. TIM lies him in bed.)

TIM
I'm getting your nurse.

(EBENEZER grabs TIM's arm.)

EBENEZER
I won't let it take you, Tim. The darkness of the world will not have you.

TIM
You have to let me go.

(EBENEZER smiles.)

EBENEZER
Never.

TIM
Uncle Ebenezer, please…

EBENEZER
…my nurse…Alice…

TIM
I'll get her.

EBENEZER
No, dammit! Listen to me…You helped save her life.

TIM
What?

EBENEZER
Years ago, we found a sick girl and…

TIM
You're not thinking clearly.

EBENEZER
Your watch! That's why she has your watch!

TIM
I don't understand.

EBENEZER
Don't you remember? Seven years ago…a street urchin tried to steal your watch. When you turned around, she collapsed in your arms.

(Beat. TIM remembers the moment.)

EBENEZER
We took her to a pub and gave her food.

TIM
She'd lost her family to a fire.

EBENEZER
Yes.

TIM
I gave her my watch.

EBENEZER
Yes, you did.

TIM
And her name was Alice.

(EBENEZER smiles.)

TIM
You're saying...That Alice...is this Alice?

EBENEZER
Yes.

TIM
My God.

EBENEZER
You want proof that something good still exists in this world? There it is! A poor, lost girl with no hope...and you gave her hope.

TIM
No. It was you who...

EBENEZER
Tim. She spoke with me tonight, told me her story. I may have gotten her off of the streets, but you saved her life.

TIM
How?

EBENEZER
You gave her your watch.

(Beat.)

TIM
That doesn't make any sense.

EBENEZER
Of course it does! It was her first gift in...I don't even know how long. Why do you think she's hung on to it all these years?

TIM
I can't imagine.

EBENEZER
Because it meant everything to her. That one thing, a small pocket watch, was what reminded her that no one is so far gone that they cannot be...redeemed.

(Beat. The truth of that hits TIM.)

EBENEZER
That's the beauty of this world, my boy. A simple act of kindness, given for no reason other than the giving...that's what changes the world.

TIM
I tried. I tried to help, and I failed.

EBENEZER
Then you try again. And again. And a thousand times more if you must. If you make even one life better, then it was worth the effort.

(MISS POOLE returns.)

MISS POOLE
What on earth is happening here?

TIM
Alice, I...

(She goes to SCROOGE, feels his head.)

MISS POOLE
Mr. Scrooge, how do you feel?

EBENEZER
Tired.

MISS POOLE
Yes, I'd imagine.

EBENEZER
And very warm.

MISS POOLE
That's not so bad a thing on as cold a night as this.
Perhaps now's the time to get some rest.

EBENEZER
Not yet.

MISS POOLE
You were waiting for a mysterious guest? Well,
here's Mister Cratchit. You two have had your fun,
but...

EBENEZER
Timothy, don't give up.

TIM
Uncle, you mustn't...

EBENEZER
Don't close your heart, as I did long ago.

MISS POOLE
Rest your eyes, sir. It's been quite a day.

(The clock outside chimes 11:45.)

EBENEZER
The bells....Timothy, the bells....

MISS POOLE
They'll be there tomorrow.

EBENEZER
If they come...you have to wake me if they come...

TIM
Who?

EBENEZER
I'm very tired.

MISS POOLE
Then sleep. And dream of Christmas morning.

(He motions TIM over. When he's near enough, EBENEZER moves him next to MISS POOLE. He then falls asleep. She goes to him.)

TIM
Is he...?

MISS POOLE
Sleeping. Just sleeping.

TIM
Will it...will it be long?

(Beat.)

MISS POOLE
I don't think so.

(TIM fights back his sorrow.)

TIM
Even at the end, he was trying to help me.

MISS POOLE
It's his way.

TIM
I should have just talked with him, remembered better times. Instead I'm nattering on about my own damn concerns and...

MISS POOLE
Mr. Cratchit, your guilt does him no good. Whatever you had to say, I'm sure he wanted to hear it.

(He sits.)

TIM
I remember you.

MISS POOLE
You do?

TIM
Now. Uncle reminded me.

MISS POOLE
Oh.

(Beat. She takes out her watch and offers it to him.)

MISS POOLE
I suppose you'd like your watch back.

(He smiles a little, shakes his head "no".)

MISS POOLE
All right then.

(She pockets it. They share an awkward beat.)

MISS POOLE
I know what kindness is now.

(He stares at her.)

MISS POOLE
When we met, all those years ago...you said I didn't know what kindness was. I do now. You taught it to me.

TIM
I did?

MISS POOLE
Yes.

TIM
But it was such a little thing, I...

MISS POOLE
Don't say that. Never say that again. I am here now, alive, because of you. And him. Thank you.

(Beat.)

MISS POOLE
The proper thing would be to say, "You're welcome."

TIM
Oh. Yes. You're welcome, of course.

(He's still very much lost in his thoughts.)

MISS POOLE
Have you seen the world?

(He stares at her.)

MISS POOLE
You were joining the Royal Navy. I imagine you've

seen many things by now.

TIM
More than I would have liked. I'm leaving the service.

MISS POOLE
Oh.

TIM
I thought the sea would show me one adventure after another.

MISS POOLE
I think we may have read the same books.

TIM
It didn't turn out like it did in the stories.

MISS POOLE
I suppose it never does.

(Beat.)

TIM
I'm glad you're here.

MISS POOLE
I'm sorry?

TIM
With him. I'm glad he's had someone with him who knew him. Someone he helped.

MISS POOLE
Oh. Well. I am a nurse. This is what I do.

TIM
It suits you. Better than pick-pocketing did, at any rate.

(She smiles.)

MISS POOLE
I was a terrible pick-pocket.

TIM
When you tried to steal that watch...

MISS POOLE
Oh god.

TIM
You might as well have introduced yourself and given me a business card.

MISS POOLE
I was that bad?

TIM
Oh yes.

MISS POOLE
Well, it was your own fault! Walking through that alley with this bit of gold just swinging from your pocket. What did you think would happen?

(He laughs a little. She smiles.)

TIM
I apologize if my being here upset you.

ALICE
It didn't.

TIM
You seemed...displeased with it earlier.

ALICE
Surprised is all.

TIM
I believe you said I wasn't conducive to my uncle's rest.

ALICE
I only meant…Mr. Cratchit…

TIM
Timothy. Please.

ALICE
Timothy…when you've had to fight your whole life, you forget that…I don't mean to push people away. I just don't know how to stop.

TIM
You're not pushing me away.

ALICE
Now. But when you came in, I…

TIM
I'm still here, and you haven't tossed me out the door.

ALICE
No. I suppose I haven't.

(Beat.)

ALICE
I'm glad you're here too.

(Suddenly, the window blows open again. The sound of the storm is louder. The lamps blow out, and the stage goes dark. A light slowly rises on EBENEZER. He bolts up from his sleep, as if waking from a dream.)

EBENEZER
Hello? Hello, who's there?

(TIM starts to laugh a little.)

EBENEZER
Who's there?!

(TIM laughs louder now, a huge laugh filling the room.)

EBENEZER
I know that laugh.

(The lights rise. TIM & MISS POOLE are still there, though their demeanors have changed. They both smile at EBENEZER, and TIM continues laughing.)

TIM
Well I'd hope so, man! Few know me better than you!

EBENEZER
You're…you're not Tim.

(He laughs again.)

TIM
Not at all! I've just borrowed him for a moment.

EBENEZER
Then you are…?

TIM
I think you know.

EBENEZER
Can you not say your own name?

TIM
Oh, I've said it so many times. Why don't you?

EBENEZER
You…you are the Ghost of Christmas Present.

(TIM laughs.)

TIM
Indeed I am!

(EBENEZER rises, suddenly full of life again. He

runs to TIM, shaking his hand vigorously.)

EBENEZER
You came! I knew you would, you see! And you...

(He goes to MISS POOLE, taking her by the shoulders. Her demeanor is more gentle & kindly.)

MISS POOLE
Christmas Past. It's so very good to see you again.

(He hugs her. She lets out a surprised shout & hugs him back.)

EBENEZER
You're here! This is glorious! Beyond glorious! Resplendent! Heavenly!

(He paces the room excitedly.)

EBENEZER
I'd almost lost hope, you see. I knew in my heart that you'd come to me again, but when it took you so long, I began to worry. I said to myself, "Ebenezer, you mustn't lose faith in..." Wait. Why are you here like this?

MISS POOLE
Like what?

EBENEZER
Why are you her? And why are you him? When we met all those years ago, you had your own forms, your own shapes.

MISS POOLE
Then, we appeared to you to take you to our respective domains. The past...

TIM
And the present.

MISS POOLE
But to step out of our realms, to appear together on the night before Christmas, we needed to borrow these mortals for the briefest of times.

EBENEZER
I didn't realize you could do that.

TIM
It's perhaps not as impressive as traveling through time, but we do find it useful, on occasion.

EBENEZER
I never realized.

MISS POOLE
Our task is to lead lost souls back to a better life. No easy thing, that.

TIM
Many consider you to be our greatest success. Well, not mine per se, but...

EBENEZER
No need to be modest. You were instrumental in my redemption.

TIM
Not me, Ebenezer. My brother.

EBENEZER
Your...brother?

TIM
Born fifteen years ago.

EBENEZER
Ah, yes! Of course! You told me this before...

TIM
Every year another Christmas Present, as it were. Ha!

EBENEZER
Over 1800 then!

TIM
The family outings can get...complicated.

EBENEZER
It was you, wasn't it? Yours were the voices I've been hearing?

MISS POOLE
Indeed.

TIM
We've been whispering to you on the wind for quite some time now.

MISS POOLE
Gently at first, reassuring you of our presence.

TIM
Speaking so quietly you barely noticed.

MISS POOLE
But as your time drew near...

TIM
So did we.

EBENEZER
But why?

MISS POOLE
We have heard the call of your soul, old friend.

TIM
What is it you want?

MISS POOLE
Your time in this world draws to a close.

EBENEZER
I know.

TIM
You've freed yourself from the chains that could have been your damnation.

EBENEZER
And I'm glad to hear it, but...

MISS POOLE
Isn't that enough?

(Beat.)

EBENEZER
No.

MISS POOLE
No?

EBENEZER
No. I want to continue.

TIM
You've lived a long life. We cannot extend it.

EBENEZER
There must be something you can do! Please! The boy whose body you inhabit...I love him as though he were my own son. His heart is broken, his hope...shattered. How could I leave this world knowing he might lose his way?

MISS POOLE
There may be a way, but it isn't a decision to be made lightly.

EBENEZER
Anything. Just tell me.

TIM
When we came to you fifteen years gone, there was another with us.

EBENEZER
Yes. Of course. The Ghost of Christmas Yet to Come.

TIM
Old Doom-&-Gloom.

MISS POOLE
Don't call him that.

EBENEZER
I feared him more than any other. But if he is to join us, I will....

TIM
He's moved on.

EBENEZER
What?

TIM
Moved on. Ascended. Gone to his eternal reward.

EBENEZER
Indeed?

MISS POOLE
Oh yes. It is the fate of all Spirits of Christmas. We serve through the years, bringing hope to those who need it most. And when our time has come, we are welcomed into the Heavenly Host.

TIM
Which is why we are here, Ebenezer.

(Beat.)

EBENEZER
What do you mean?

TIM
We who were once three are now only two.

MISS POOLE
And there must always be three.

MISS POOLE
So join us, Ebenezer Scrooge.

(Beat.)

EBENEZER
You...you mean, as a ghost?

TIM
Not just any ghost.

EBENEZER
The Ghost of Christmas Yet To Come?

MISS POOLE
Yes. But know this; it is no small thing, being a Ghost of Christmas.

EBENEZER
I know.

MISS POOLE
Do you? With each passing year, the world grows colder, men's hearts grow darker, and kindness drifts further from their minds.

TIM
When we came to you fifteen Christmases ago, you retook your own life, and tried to do some good with it. Many have not.

EBENEZER
How many have you visited? How many like me?

MISS POOLE
More than you can imagine. Many turn us away.

TIM
And with each rejection, our light dims in this world.

MISS POOLE
You have seen the desperation of the past.

TIM
And the desolation of the present.

MISS POOLE
Do you truly wish to join our ranks? To light a single candle against the growing darkness?

EBENEZER
Of course. Of course I do.

MISS POOLE
Why?

EBENEZER
Because one candle can light another, and another, and another.

(Beat. TIM laughs.)

TIM
An excellent answer, Mr. Scrooge. A most excellent answer.

EBENEZER
Then you will have me? I can join you?

MISS POOLE
It's why we came here, to make you this very offer.

(He shakes their hands.)

EBENEZER
Thank you! Oh joyous day!

MISS POOLE
There is much you will have to learn.

EBENEZER
Of course. Absolutely.

TIM
We haven't had a new Christmas Yet To Come in…
well, since before I started.

EBENEZER
Then it's true. I am to become…the future?

MISS POOLE
Yes. Your story will live on and on, further than
you can imagine.

TIM
Three hundred years from now, they will still
know the name Ebenezer Scrooge. Parents will
tell their children of the hard-hearted, miserly
wretch…

EBENEZER
All right.

TIM
…who found his soul one Christmas Day.

EBENEZER
That…I cannot thank you enough.

MISS POOLE
Come.

(The window opens.)

MISS POOLE
Your body will remain here. Your spirit will come with us.

EBENEZER
Just...just one more thing.

TIM
The clock is ticking, Ebenezer.

EBENEZER
I wish to be a... different sort of ghost.

MISS POOLE
Oh?

EBENEZER
My predecessor... Old Doom-&-Gloom.... he relied on fear and shadows.

MISS POOLE
It was most effective, if I recall.

EBENEZER
Of course, but...

MISS POOLE
If a method is proven effective, I see no need to change it.

EBENEZER
My friends...when mankind fears the future, they accomplish...nothing. They turn on each other, and finally themselves, and wonder where it all went wrong. I think perhaps I'd like to try a different approach.

MISS POOLE
Every new partner has their own ideas on how to improve the business, but...

TIM
HA!

MISS POOLE
What?

TIM
Oh come now! You were the worst of all of us!

MISS POOLE
That's ridiculous.

TIM
Do not forget, I share the memory of all my brothers before me. Your first day, you came in with your changing forms and your flying through windows and...

MISS POOLE
You're exaggerating.

TIM
Old Doom-&-Gloom was spitting fire! And what did my brother tell him? Hmm?

(MISS POOLE mumbles something.)

TIM
I must have missed that.

MISS POOLE
He said "Each spirit is chosen for a reason, and we should honor that."

TIM
Yes. I believe that's the gist of it.

(TIM goes to EBENEZER.)

TIM
So you don't want to bring them fear?

EBENEZER
No. A man shouldn't change for fear of the punish-
ment.

TIM
Then what shall you bring them?

EBENEZER
Hope.

(TIM smiles at that.)

TIM
Hope. Now that has some potential. Wouldn't you
agree?

MISS POOLE
We can try it.

(She motions to the bed.)

EBENEZER
I don't understand.

MISS POOLE
It's as I said, Ebenezer. Your spirit will join us. But
your body...

EBENEZER
Remains here.

(He stares at the bed, afraid.)

EBENEZER
Will it hurt?

TIM
Not at all. You'll simply fall asleep.

EBENEZER
And never awaken.

MISS POOLE
You will awaken. With us. And you will begin your
good work.

EBENEZER
I want that. More than anything. But...

TIM
Fear is a natural thing, especially at a moment like
this. But there is something stronger than fear, isn't
there?

(EBENEZER smiles at him.)

EBENEZER
Yes there is.

*(EBENEZER lies on the bed. MISS POOLE goes
to him.)*

MISS POOLE
I have a gift for you, old friend.

EBENEZER
You do?

MISS POOLE
Soon, you shall see the future before you in all its
infinite variety. Would you like a glimpse at what
is yet to come?

EBENEZER
Oh yes. Yes, very much.

*(She puts her hand on his head. The lights go out. In
the darkness, the clock tolls midnight. The lamps soon
relight themselves, and TIM & MISS POOLE are
back to where they were before they were possessed.
The window is now shut. EBENEZER's eyes are
open. He smiles.)*

EBENEZER
Oh my. How…wondrous.

(He passes away.)

TIM
Uncle Ebenezer?

(MISS POOLE goes to him. She checks his pulse.)

TIM
Is he…

(She closes his eyes, then pulls the sheet over him. TIM finally cries. MISS POOLE goes to him. She is tentative at first, but puts her arms around him.)

MISS POOLE
There's no shame in your tears. Just means that you loved him.

TIM
Everyone loved him.

MISS POOLE
Would you like a moment? Alone, I mean? I have to…

(He takes her hand.)

TIM
Please don't go.

MISS POOLE
I won't.

(They are silent for a bit.)

MISS POOLE
He was waiting for ghosts.

(He stares at her.)

MISS POOLE
I'm sorry. I don't mean to sound morbid. Only that...he said that ghosts were coming. At midnight.

TIM
Maybe they're here, and we just can't see them.

MISS POOLE
There's a thought.

(TIM goes to EBENEZER. He places a hand on his shoulder.)

TIM
Wherever you are now, Uncle...God bless you.

(The window blows open again. MISS POOLE, startled, goes to TIM & takes his hand. EBENEZER's voice can be heard singing, and from their reactions, it's clear that TIM & MISS POOLE can hear him.)

EBENEZER
And all the bells on Earth shall ring on Christmas Day, on Christmas Day

And all the souls on Earth shall sing on Christmas Day in the morning

(Lights fade.)

END OF PLAY

ABOUT THE PLAYWRIGHT

Joseph Zettelmaier is a Michigan-based playwright and four-time nominee for the Steinberg/American Theatre Critics Association Award for best new play, first in 2006 for *All Childish Things*, then in 2007 for *Language Lessons*, in 2010 for *It Came From Mars* and in 2012 for *Dead Man's Shoes*. Other plays include *Salvage, The Gravedigger, Northern Aggression, Dr. Seward's Dracula, All Childish Things, Invasive Species, Dead Man's Shoes, The Scullery Maid, Night Blooming and Ebenezer. Point of Origin* won Best Locally Created Script 2002 from the Ann Arbor News, and *The Stillness Between Breaths* also won Best New Play 2005 from the Oakland Press. *The Stillness Between Breaths* and *It Came From Mars* were selected to appear in the National New Play Network's Festival of New Plays. He also co-authored Flyover, USA: Voices From Men of the Midwest at the Williamston Theatre (Winner of the 2009 Thespie Award for Best New Script). He also adapted *Christmas Carol'd* for the Performance Network. *It Came From Mars* was a recipient of 2009's Edgerton Foundation New American Play Award, and won Best New Script 2010 from the Lansing State Journal. His play *Dead Man's Shoes* won the Edgerton Foundation New American Play Award in 2011. He is an Associate Artist at First Folio Shakespeare, an Artistic Ambassador to the National New Play Network, and an adjunct lecturer at Eastern Michigan University, where he teaches Dramatic Composition.

PLAYS FROM SORDELET INK

IT CAME FROM MARS
by Joseph Zettelmaier

EBENEEZER
by Joseph Zettelmaier

THE MOONSTONE
by Robert Kauzlaric
based on the novel by Wilkie Collins

EVE OF IDES
by David Blixt